It's Not Catching

Tooth Decay

Heinemann
LIBRARY

Angela Royston

www.heinemann.co.uk/library
Visit our website to find out more information about **Heinemann Library** books.

To order:
☎ Phone 44 (0) 1865 888066
🖹 Send a fax to 44 (0) 1865 314091
🖥 Visit the Heinemann Bookshop at www.heinemann.co.uk/library to browse our catalogue and order online.

First published in Great Britain by Heinemann Library, Halley Court, Jordan Hill, Oxford OX2 8EJ, part of Harcourt Education.
Heinemann is a registered trademark of Harcourt Education Ltd.

Editorial: Sarah Eason and Kathy Peltan
Design: Dave Oakley, Arnos Design
Picture Research: Helen Reilly, Arnos Design
Artwork: Nick Hawken p. 11; Tower designs UK p. 14
Production: Edward Moore

Originated by Dot Gradations Ltd.
Printed and bound in Hong Kong and China by South China Printing Company

The paper used to print this book comes from sustainable sources.

ISBN 0 431 02146 5
08 07 06 05 04
10 9 8 7 6 5 4 3 2 1

British Library Cataloguing in Publication Data
Royston, Angela
Tooth decay. – (It's not catching)
617.6'7

A full catalogue record for this book is available from the British Library.

Acknowledgements
The publishers would like to thank the following for permission to reproduce photographs:
Corbis Stock p. **29**; Eyewire p. **7**; Gareth Boden p. **13**; Getty Images/Dave Nagel p. **4**; Getty Images/Stone/Bruce Ayres p. **28**; Phillip James Photography pp. **5, 8, 9, 11, 15, 18, 19, 20, 21, 25**; Powerstock p. **26**; Powerstock/Oote Boe p. **17**; SPL p. **10**; SPL/BSIP p. **3, SPL/BSIP/VEM** p. **14**; SPL/CNRI p. **12**; SPL/James King-Holmes p. **16**; Trevor Clifford pp. **6, 22, 23, 24, 27**.

Cover photograph reproduced with permission of Tudor Photography.

The publishers would like to thank David Wright for his assistance in the preparation of this book.

Every effort has been made to contact copyright holders of any material reproduced in this book. Any omissions will be rectified in subsequent printings if notice is given to the publishers.

Contents

Words written in bold, **like this**, are explained in the Glossary.

What is tooth decay?

Healthy teeth are covered with a hard substance called **enamel**. Tooth decay begins when you get a small hole in the enamel on one of your teeth.

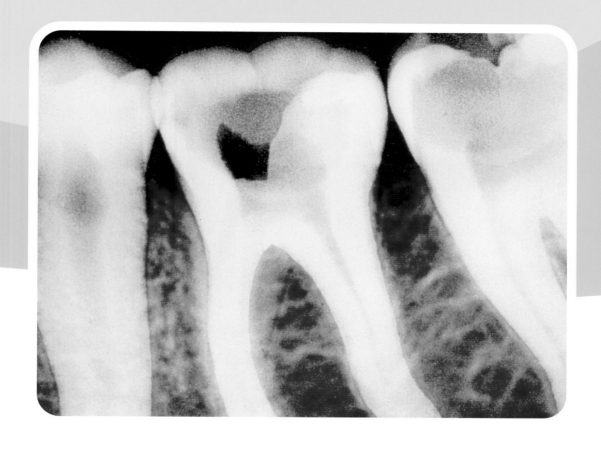

You may not feel anything until the hole becomes deeper. If the hole reaches the middle of your tooth, you get a very painful toothache.

Who gets tooth decay?

Anyone can get tooth decay. How likely you are to get tooth decay depends mainly on how you look after yourself. You cannot catch tooth decay from someone else.

You will get tooth decay if you do not look after your teeth. People who are always eating and drinking sweet things are likely to get tooth decay.

What causes tooth decay?

Sugar causes tooth decay. Some foods are particularly sweet. Sweet snacks, such as sweets, chocolate, cakes and biscuits, all contain a lot of sugar.

Fizzy drinks, such
as lemonade and cola,
contain a lot of sugar too.
When you eat or drink
sugary things, some of the
sugar is left in your mouth.

Sugar causes tooth decay

bacteria seen through
a microscope

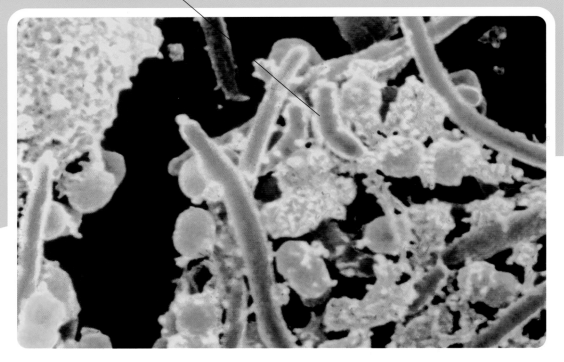

Millions of tiny **bacteria** live in your mouth.
They are too small to see except through a
microscope. The bacteria feed on the sugar
left in your mouth.

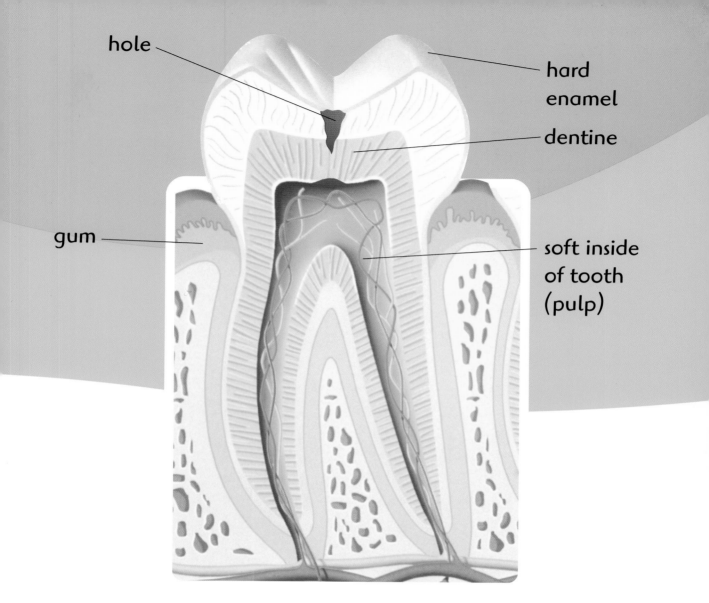

hole

hard
enamel

dentine

gum

soft inside
of tooth
(pulp)

As they feed, they produce an **acid**. The acid
burns holes in the **enamel** covering your
teeth. The acid then begins to destroy the
dentine below.

Gum disease

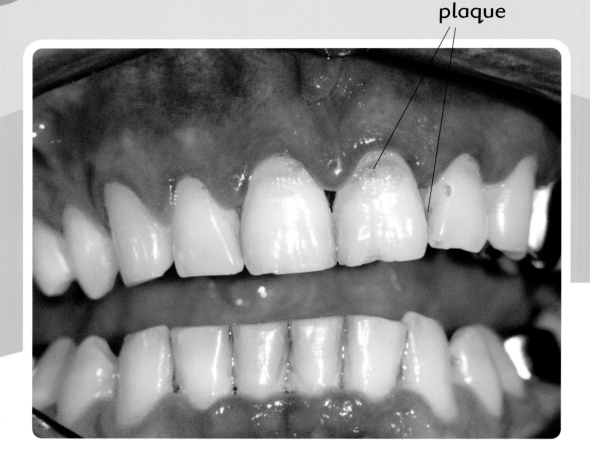

plaque

Bacteria and sugary food in the mouth form a sticky, paste, called **plaque**. Plaque gets trapped between your teeth and your **gums**. It also builds up between your teeth.

The bacteria in plaque attack your teeth and can **irritate** your gums. Sore gums bleed easily. Bacteria that get under your gums can form a painful **abscess**.

severe toothache

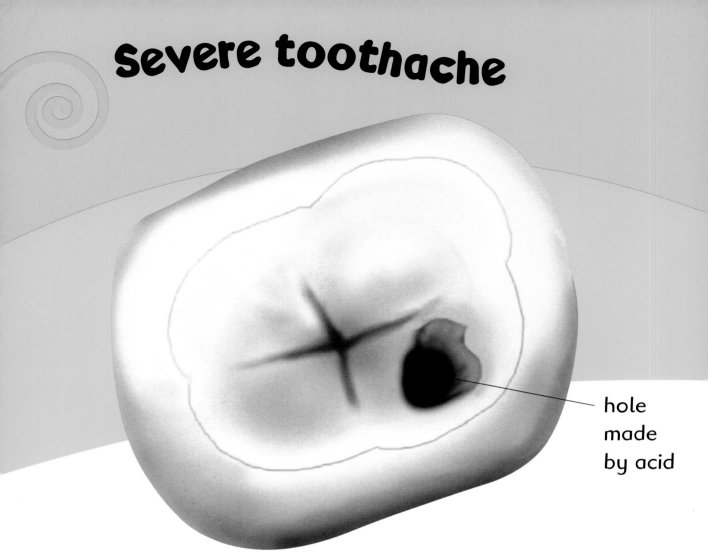

hole
made
by acid

Dentine is not as strong as the **enamel** that
covers each tooth. The **acid** that causes tooth
decay can soon eat its way through dentine
to the **pulp**.

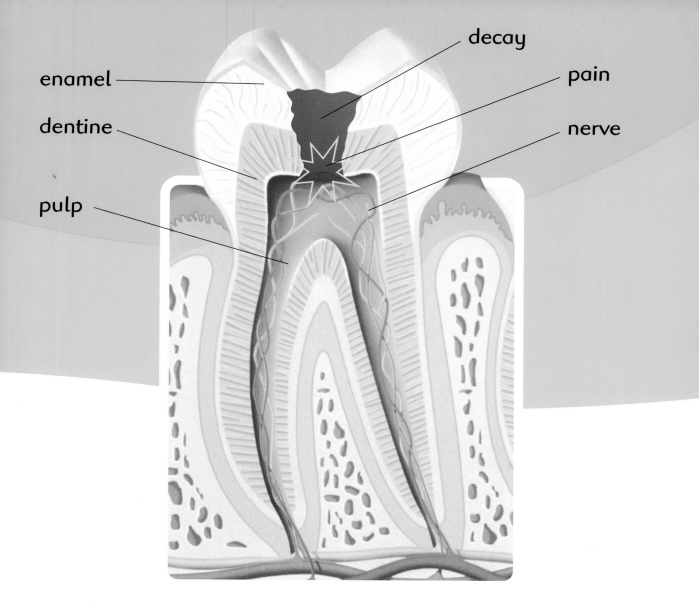

enamel

dentine

pulp

decay

pain

nerve

The pulp in the centre of the tooth contains
nerves and blood. As the hole gets deeper, it
causes very painful toothache. The pain tells
you that something is wrong.

Treating tooth decay

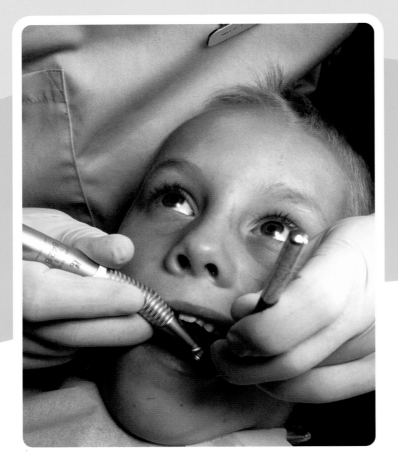

A **dentist** uses a **drill** to get rid of all the rotten bits of tooth. But first the dentist gives you an **anaesthetic** so that you do not feel anything.

filling

Now your tooth has a much bigger hole! But the remaining tooth is healthy. The dentist fills the hole with a mixture of special chemicals, called a **filling**.

Treating gum disease

The way to cure **gum** disease is to rinse your mouth with **antiseptic** mouthwash. You have to rinse your mouth for a few minutes in the morning and at night.

People who have an **abscess** have to take
an **antibiotic** medicine. The medicine kills
the **germs** that cause the infection. The
dentist may then take the tooth out.

Cleaning your teeth

Cleaning your teeth helps to prevent tooth decay. You should clean your teeth after meals, in the morning and last thing at night. Use toothpaste and a toothbrush.

Dental floss is a thin string that helps to get rid of **plaque**. Your **dentist** will show you how to use the floss to clean between your teeth and **gums** when you are older.

Brushing your teeth

Brush each tooth from the **gum** to the tip of the tooth. Brush the back of each tooth as well as the front. Then brush the tops of your back teeth.

A toothbrush only lasts for a few months. Then the bristles become soft and spread out, like this. An old toothbrush will not clean your teeth properly.

Healthy food

Some foods help to make your teeth strong and healthy. Eating raw carrots, celery and apple helps to clean your teeth. They are much healthier than sweets and chocolate!

Milk, cheese and yoghurt contain a
substance called **calcium**. Your teeth
contain calcium too. Eating plenty of
calcium makes your teeth extra strong.

Fluoride

Fluoride makes your teeth so strong that they are much less likely to decay. In some places, a small amount of fluoride is added to the drinking water.

If your tap water has no fluoride, you can take fluoride as drops, tablets, mouthwash or in toothpaste. Ask your **dentist** first, because too much fluoride can discolour your teeth.

Dental check-ups

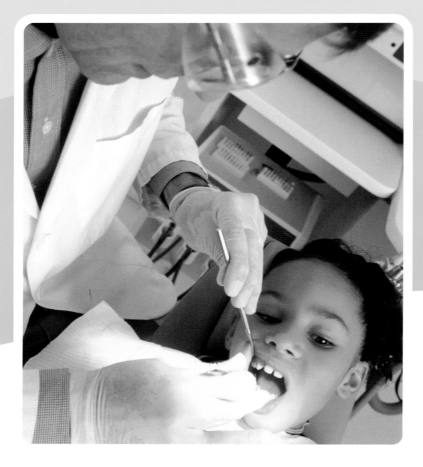

You should visit the **dentist** every six months to have your teeth checked. The dentist examines your teeth to see if there is any tooth decay or **gum** disease.

The dentist may coat your teeth with a **sealant** to help prevent decay. Make sure you look after your second set of teeth. They have to last your whole life!

Glossary

abscess part of the skin or gums which is swollen and sore because it is infected by germs

acid bitter or sour liquid that can burn holes in teeth

anaesthetic something that makes you lose all feeling, particularly the feeling of pain

antibiotic medicine that cures infections caused by bacteria

antiseptic something that stops bacteria growing

bacteria type of germ

calcium mineral that makes your teeth and bones strong and hard

dental floss special thread that you use between your teeth and gums to get rid of plaque

dentine hard part of the tooth below the enamel

dentist person who is trained to take care of teeth and repair damaged teeth

drill instrument for making holes

enamel very hard, shiny substance that covers the surface of a tooth

filling chemicals that are used to fill holes in the teeth

fluoride   mineral that makes your teeth more able to resist decay

germs   tiny living things, such as bacteria, that can cause disease if they get inside your body

gums   flesh that covers your jaw bones and the roots of your teeth

infection   disease caused by germs

irritate   make sore

microscope   instrument that makes very small things look big enough to see

plaque   white paste that builds up between your teeth and under your gums

pulp   soft substance at the centre of a tooth

sealant   substance that makes something airtight and watertight

More books to read

Look After Yourself: Healthy Teeth, Angela Royston, (Heinemann Library, 2003)

Body Matters: Why Do I Get Toothache? And Other Questions about Nerves, Angela Royston, (Heinemann Library, 2002)

Index